In Shamballah

A collection of poetry

by K.M. O'Connor

In Shamballah, a collection of poetry

by K.M. O'Connor

First edition

Published by Kula Comms. Ltd, 2011

ISBN 978-0-9571293-0-6

By the same author:

Put this parsnip on your nose! a collection of nonsense rhymes and verse for children

For more information visit:
www.inshamballah.co.uk

As well as writing poetry for adults, Kenneth O'Connor has written numerous nonsense rhymes and verses for children. Some of these were featured on BBC Radio's 4 Poetry Corner and in accompanying booklets for schools during the 1970s. Others were published in a children's collection entitled Sit on the Roof and Holler edited by Adrian Rumble and published by Puffin Books in 1984. Some of his Haiku verses were also featured in the highly acclaimed Spam-ku: Tranquil Reflections on Luncheon Loaf by John Cho published in the US by Harper Perennial in 1998.

In 2011 his family brought together their favourite of his children's poems under the title: *Put this parsnip on your nose! a collection of nonsense rhymes and verse for children.*

ABOUT THE AUTHOR

Born in Burma between the wars, Kenneth Michael O'Connor was educated by Jesuit priests at Clongowes Wood College in Ireland and Beaumont College in England. Like many children of his generation, whose parents lived in far-flung places around a fading British Empire, he missed his parents and longed for family life.

Medically discharged from the armed forces during WWII, he went on to study art at St Marylebone's School of Art in London. Kenneth and his other discharged friends spent much of their time living a bohemian lifestyle in Chelsea, dodging bombs and surviving on their wits and humour. This lively and carefree, albeit penniless time fuelled his interest in people and his talent as an artist and poet. When he met Jean in 1955 Kenneth said he had finally found real meaning in his life and asked her to be his wife. Abandoning the bohemian life, Kenneth married Jean and together they successfully went on to build the large and loving family he had always yearned for.

To Jean

TABLE OF CONTENTS

Contents continued overleaf .../...

INSPIRATION

It is essential
To be very still.
In due course
Mind opens a window
Cautiously,
Slowly. Slowly
Something enters.
Something?
An intruder?
A thingamajig?
Thing looks around,
Reaches into itself
And spatters coloured stuff
All over
Visions, ideas, songs,
Stories, jokes, etc.
Some of the stuff is ok.
The rest is decoration.
Thing goes out, exhausted.
Mind slams the shutters.
Cleans up!

SHAMBALLAH

Shamballah is not on Mount Merou,
nor in Agartha
But in a disused air-raid shelter,
Down ten stone steps, steeply turning
Under a rockery in my garden.

With permission, with discretion
You can enter Shamballah.
In the damp earth scented darkness
You can stand and be aware
Without regard to ancient ritual
You can in time become aware.

What massive thoughts are these
That burn as suns across what galaxies?
Whose hands are those that catch and fold
Cascading planes of time and space
Around this transient mould?

Later, when they come to take you

From the darkness of that cellar,

When they lead you gently down my garden,

White coated guardians holding firmly,

You will whisper 'Shamballah'.

WIFE

Similes escape.
It is enough
Sensing your innocence,
Floating pleasantly
Through tranquil seas'
Sharing memories,
Cool and clear,
Wavelets lapping,
Like childhood.

Similes escape.
Enough it is,
Sensing your presence,
Feeling internally
A gentle immanence.
Subtle resonances
Of soul, of mind
Permeate constantly
Like childhood.

TO JEAN

Theorem of Pythagoras, the blackbird's song,
Wing sweep of a gull in flight, river mist
Broken by the morning sun. Our words,
Poor cages, cannot capture these,
Only their faint reflections. And yet,
Simply by touching your soul, I know
The real shape of all these things.

RECOGNITION

Mind vacant,
Sipping café-latte,
The laser sears my neck
Intense blue eyebeams
From a pink blob
In a carrycot.
I return the stare
Without expression,
Unblinking,
Merciless.
Pinky gears down.
Eyeballs surrender.
The brain retreats.
Memories regress
Until I too
Am six months old.
In mutual recognition
We smile.

CHAOS

Like an improbable
Candelabrum,
Prisms and flamelets
In dark rooms drifting,
The mind illuminates
Objects inconsequential.

Perceptions of infinity
Available only
At the witching second
'Twixt night and sunrise,
Seen upside down
In a water meadow.

Curtains of chaos
Contrive together
For our delight.
Kissing hands forever,
Leaving and greeting
In humorous abandon.

FABLE 1

Decrepit, the old skin bag drags his feet,
Balanced precariously
On wobbly knees. He sags insidiously
In unexpected places. Inside
The ancient tendons twang and creak
Like plaintive mandolins.
'For goodness sake' they sing
'Sit you down and take a seat.

Stretched out upon the sofa, he burps
Softly, surreptitiously at first,
Then louder, as in distant thunder.
Once more he strains
But nothing comes, no, not one fragrant whisper.
'Ah well' he sighs 'The story of my life
Set to music'.

FABLE 2

There is nothing to it really.
Wholeness, holding hands,
Gull swoops, eye swoons,
Fragrances, primal rhythms,
Let them come, strive not.
Loving oozes up, surrounds and swirls.
One balances and pirouettes in vain.
Don't strain.
Wise men walk widdershins.

FABLE 3

There are no heliotropes in my garden
Or anywhere in these places
(And yet, and yet)
No rhododendrons, cassia plants.
Who cares?
But somewhere, quite definitely,
I know you are there.

Perhaps, if spinning suddenly,
Like a manic clown gyrating,
I'll see you magic Columbine
From the eyes' corner
Elegantly disappearing, yet leaving
The unmistakable scent of heliotropes.

TRIBAL ELDER

Rather slow move the bones, now,
And the abdomen lacks suspension.
Heart and head, however, fly,
As eagles, soaring, exploring
Pastures of mind, perceptions of spirits.

No longer able
To draw a hunting bow,
To throw my sharp spear,
Or to track the swift deer,
Content am I,
To take a privileged place,
And eat the choicest portions,
To enjoy my woman and her children.

BETTER THAN

Honest, really,
Next to cuddling
And eating,
Comes paddling
In sea water
On clean sandy beaches.
Friendly ripples
Caress
Ankle height.
Toes explore
Hospitable sands..
Senses
Exhilarate.
Sea birds,
Sea breezes
Accompany.
It's all more subtle
Than just
Swimming.

INSPRATION 1

Aaaargh!
One can feel it now,
Buzzing between the toes,
Slithering up the abdomen
Resting in one's warm fork.
Wow!
It darts, that frenetic entity,
Like a mad intestinal whirligig
And finally comes to rest.
Ass in my heart,
Fizz in my head.
That's the way it always is.

A COW

Consider this cow.
Be not deceived
By her facade
Of dumb complacency.
This cow is an alien,
Incredibly intelligent,
Of superior genesis.
With devious cunning
She exploits our shelters,
Pastures and devotions.

Meanwhile,
Absorbing nourishment
Directly from the planet,
I say 'be not deceived'.
Look into this cow's eyes,
They are not blank
Like a sheep's,
Nor subservient
Like some dogs,
Nor inscrutable

Like a cat's.

A cow's eyes are

Dark unfathomable entrances

To a distant universe.

Beware!!

ANGEL

It's no picnic being an archangel
With all that crazy stuff
Which goes with the territory.
It's not just sidetracking sinners
From inevitable perdition
Or keeping saints and cherubs in line.
It's the whole archaic infrastructure
Which is so undermining.
Taking out my golden trumpet
Early this aeon, I found it clogged up
With angelic ectoplasm; doubtless,
The work of an intrusive imp.
Today, flying to take up position
On the front bench of the heavenly choir,
I fluttered around in manic circles.
Some mischievous spirit had stuck
Angel cake to my wing.
I am a Seraphim, you know,
And need to maintain appearances.
I'm not a moaner usually but please
Put in a word with the Boss.

DEITY

Hello God.
It must be fun
Constantly creating everything,
Dimensions, galaxies, universes
And all that big stuff.
And yet,
As the magicians say.
'As above so below'.
Even now, as I write,
Unimaginably minute
Subatomic quantum bits
Rupture time,
Appearing and disappearing
Like cosmic acrobats.
Some saints, artists and scientists
Can detect your hand
Behind it all
And draw aside the curtains of illusion
An infinitesimal bit,
Exposing beauty.

AUTUMN

A frosty night in
November.
Above the garden
Stars parade,
Galaxies twirl,
Black holes vacuum
Regardless.

Eyes shut.

Scents of damp stone.
Leaf mould and
Old bonfires
Pervade.
Blackbirds scold
A stealthy cat.
Distant children chatter.
Overhead,
Occasional passenger jets
Drone robotically.

Eyes open.

A streetlamp casts
Sharp coniferous shadows
Against the frosted lawn.
Fireworks erupt like flowers
Above cut-out chimney tops

Great!

TIME SHIFT

Like placid evasive
Ingratiating conmen;
Weeks follow weeks,
Slipping by smoothly
With coffee at breakfast.

Perpetual Saturdays
Appear with apologies.
Only newspapers
Remark the passages
Inconsequential.

Strung between weekends,
Bright beads on a necklace,
Breaking time sequence,
Sparkling happenings
Illuminate history.

That's what it was about.
That's what it is about.
Love makes the world go round.
And that's the truth.

WORDS

Words don't grow seedling slow,

Elegantly uncoiling, stretching.

In fact, like cherry pips, they slip at speed,

Propelled by pulsing fissures in the heads

Of politicians, priests and poets.

REALITY

This October morning,
Prostrate on a new mattress,
After a good sleep
And a really hot cuppa
I feel resolved.
'Wow' I say
To my well-worn body bits.
'We really are part
Of the whole works.
Our mineral elements
Were created
In galactic supernovae
Billions of years ago,
Same as those
In the garden foxes
And sociable daisies'.

‘So what?’ old body replied
‘Get out of bed.
Make me a breakfast of
Bacon and eggs,
Sauté potatoes
And grated molybdenum
Molecules.’

DROPOUT

Bitter song feast, wishbone broken,
Soaked with pot and soul bespoken,
You wear the mystic mask of Christ.
Gold rimmed specs and tinted glass
To hide those Jesus eyes.

HALLOWEEN

Mad as a moon bug, mad am I.

Splittering, spluttering-spit in your eye.

Skittering, skuttering, running at night.

Treading old bones, screaming with fright

Fires of lost souls searing the air.

Hands in the darkness, clawing your hair.

Lord of the loonies let there be light.

VAMPIRES

Down the streets
The young girls go
White, white skin
As cold dry snow.
Left knee up and
Right foot down,
All around the
Moonlit town.

Oh come, come quick
By the casement there.
He's tall and dark,
Sweet cavalier.
His blood is rich,
so red and strong.
They'll not keep him
very long.

TRIAL

"A little bit derivative"
The Art Master cried
And scribbled on my virgin mind
Until it had died.

"A little bit inquisitive".
The Head Master winced
And sliced up my severed soul
Until it was minced.

"A little bit inhibited".
The Great God smiled
And kissed me on the forehead
Until I was healed.

CONVENT OPEN DAY

Sentinel poplars stand tall
And prim. Under their shade
Self conscious parents drift
In clusters, sipping orangeade.
The still warm air, heavy
With scents of new mown grass
And eager adolescence pervades.

Suddenly, like apparitions,
Three ancient nuns appear.
Black cloaks flapping, they tack
Across the lawn, swinging about,
Hard-a-starboard, and bear down
Upon our unprotected flank
Nonplussed, we float, dismasted,
Among the pink piranhas of our prime,
And reluctantly succumb to sandwiches
And teatime.

ELINOR

'Come into my house' the old man said.
His head was made of wood, his heart from lead.

The girl at the gate stood on her tiptoes.
'I might' she sighed 'I might, I suppose'.

The old man's eyes were two red stones.
Of candle wax his long white bones.

'We can have cold tea and mouldy bread
And stale mince pies' the old man said.

'I don't mind if I do' said Elinor
And followed him through the great oak door.

No one has seen her anymore!

THE DOG

Happened this dog
Sitting on my morning bed
Near enough 5.30 am.
Smelling of old boots and shoe polish.
Sitting there, a black intruder.
(A Doberman cum Rottweiler).
Licking his privates
And chewing my slipper,
A ridiculous false tongue.

'Ho there, big fellah' I said.
The dog looked at me and grinned.
He grunted and the bedsprings hummed
Like seismic sensors.
How did this canine freak arrive?
Maybe I'm stuck with it,
Having to find enormous meals
And take it on arduous marathons.
It's mid-noon now and he's still there,
Looking hungry.
What the Hell am I to do?

THE FOOT

'Finely tuned am I
Echoing nuances
Of past pilgrimages.
(Left foot this,
Toes outstretched cat-wise
On Bognor beach,
Sand between toes)
To be sea cleansed and wave caressed.
And then,
Sockless on an April lawn,
To sense the new mown grass.
To be a foot
Is good.'

Day ends.
A cradle of vintage slippers
Awaits.

A TRUE STORY

There was this snail,
By name Samuel,
Crawling, crawling
Up the North Face
Of the Bank of England,
Threadneedle Street, London.
Unfortunately, I say unfortunately,
A passing pouter pigeon,
Montmorency,
Spotted Samuel
On his way up
To the Governor's
Open casement window,
Where stood
An attractive but vulnerable
Aspidistra.
'Wow' thought Monty,
Who was something of a gourmet
'L'escargot on the shell'.
Executing a neat Immelman turn,
He zoomed in swiftly
On succulent Samuel.

However, Sam,

Who was not born yesterday,

Leapt aside with agility,

As molluscs are prone to do

Under stress

And scampered up

The precipitous face

Of The North aspect

Of the Bank of England,

Hiding safely under

The Governor's aspidistra.

Meanwhile, I say meanwhile,

Monty,

Unable to change direction in mid flight

Cricked his neck badly

And has had to fly at an angle of 45 degrees

To his final destination

Ever since.

Perhaps there is a moral to this story-

Somewhere.

CUTLASS

Gazing fondly in the mirror,
Cutlass the house cat
Stropped and honed his claws
Ostentatiously. He grinned,
Displaying formidable incisors and
Needle point canine teeth.
‘Ahhrr’ he purred
‘Really, I’m rather terrifyingly terrific’.
Changing posture, in slow motion,
He gave a repeat performance.
‘Gad’ he hissed
‘How I do love me’. Meanwhile,
Manfred the mouse, his sister Clothilde,
His cousin Zak and
A friendly cockroach, Charley,
Carried away and otherwise
Consumed at leisure
Half a peanut butter sandwich,
A chocolate sponge fancy cake,
Two thirds of a knackwurst sausage
And a mouldy black shoe lace.

Mrs Eliza Simmons,
Owner of 41 Railway Cuttings,
Was hugely proud of Cutlass the cat.
One could see he was rather magnificent.
In due course skeletal Mrs Simmons
Passed away with food poisoning
And number 41 gently collapsed,
Quite eaten away.

CARACTACUS THE CRANE

Caractacus the Crane
Stood on one leg.
Which leg it was
One could only guess.
Anyway, sideways
He looked like a question mark.
Thoughtful fish in passing
Stopped to wonder which leg?
They were snapped up quickly
By crafty Caractacus.
However, one day,
Ethelbert, an electric eel,
Happened by
And was lost in analytic process.
'Maybe' he thought 'It's the left leg.
Or, perhaps, it's the right?'
He was in mid thought,
When Caractacus snapped him up.

‘Eeeeek’ Caractacus shrieked,
Turning a triple back-flip somersault,
All feathers extended,
He landed upside down,
Scintillating blue and red
Like a neon sign
In Piccadilly Circus.
These days,
Walking by the riverside,
Should you happen to notice
A scruffy hunting crane
Standing on one leg,
Wearing a fully insulated
Rubber wellington boot,
You will know why.

ELEGANCE

Elephant footstep.
Feline posture.
Equine rhythm.
Lemur flow.
Condor glide.
Raven strut.
Springbok leap.
Lion poise.
Enjoy, enjoy.
Absorb.
Resonate.
Contemplate.
Peace be with you.

SUCCESS

My cousin, Everard,
Like Saladin,
Was able to slice through a cushion
In one swipe.
Furthermore, he could decapitate
Six beer bottles
Simultaneously
In a similar fashion.
However,
His wife, Jeanine,
Beat him with ease
Playing snooker, darts
And shove-halfpenny.

Their teenage son, Bert,
Was not impressed or overawed
By these puerile attempts
To prove superiority,
As he was able
To swallow a pint of lager
In less than ten seconds
While reciting
'Under Milk Wood'.

THITHER I WANDERED

Thither I wandered
(Whether I wit)
Whenever I went
Wanted to sit.

Wanted to sit
(Thinking some thinks,
Singing soft songs).
Take forty winks.

Waking betimes
(Whenever before)
Drumming of drums,
Premonitions of war.

Waking betimes
(Whatever the odds)
Imprecations of crows,
Depredations of dogs.

HATES

An idiot's guffaw,
A slamming back door,
The smell of old socks,
Encrusted padlocks,
A dripping wet nose,
Cold cramps in the toes,
Transparent small lies,
An unpleasant surprise,
The morning's cold toast,
A bill in the post,
A slimy damp hand,
A Bombay brass band,
Un-chilled lager beer,
A counterfeit tear,
Cold feet in the bed,
New warts on the head,
A fool in full cry,
A sty in the eye.

These things I abhor,
While I think of some more.

MY MIND

What is my mind like, really?
Perhaps it is an ancient attic room
Full of untidy books, covered in dust,
Some tattered and well thumbed,
Others with shiny new outrageous covers.
Through the west window
A broad shaft of gold sunlight
Filters through, constantly changing
Its pattern to the whim of dancing leaves
And bizarre exotic insects.
But in another corner
A quantum magic persists,
As, from a chink in the eastern eaves,
Probing fingers of silver luminescence
Penetrate the local darkness
Revealing forgotten artifacts.
In the very centre of my mind's room
A crystalline core persists, reflecting both gold and silver,

Yet, in itself, iridescent blue green.

All that I know for sure is that this core is the focus

Of my feelings, my thoughts and my belief.

MOMENTS

Some moments
Are memorable:
Different senses absorb
The cawing of distant crows,
The scent of new damp stones,
First shocks of cold sea,
First young caress,
First songs.
Moments to seize and keep
In a sacred place.

When perceptions still and feet stumble,
When flagging limbs fail and fingers fumble,
These moments remain.
Quanta experiences,
Measurements of life.

REFLECTIONS

Pity about the bone aches,
Mind lapses, the staggers.
The rest is good enough.

Nuances of sound and colour,
Subtle and various,
Ambience excellent.

Feelings reflect colours,
Memory modulated,
Oldest deep, newest bright.

Loving un-changed,
Like sounds and colours.
That's the best part.

PILGRIMAGE

Aspiring warriors
Must endure the rites
Of skill and survival
Before admittance.

Later, manhood proven
By combat and competence,
They must stand alone
Before the magic wildwood.

When the 'Green Man' beckons
They must follow with courage
Along a long and dangerous path
To knowledge or oblivion.

BEAT

So tired,
So tired, so tired.
Eyelids heavy,
Oh so heavy
Flaccid facades.
Mosaiced
Crimson globes
Rotate restlessly,
Seeking escape.
Oh Lord,
Oh personal
Archangel,
Send me a bed,
Soft and gentle.
An innocent's kiss.
A tender womb
For ever.
Amen.

EPITAPH

Your Spring is sprung.
Your Fling is flung.
Your Race is run.
Your Songs all sung.

Now is the Kiss.
Septennial Bliss.
Now is the Ever,
Never-never and Forever.

You lie on your back
And look at the sun
You count to three
And Doings done.

www.ingramcontent.com/pod-product-compliance
Ingram Content Group UK Ltd.
Pitfield, Milton Keynes, MK11 3LW, UK
UKHW020217250726
13967UKWH00001B/46

9 780957 129306